Robert Browning

Prince Hohenstiel-Schwangau

Saviour of Society

Robert Browning

Prince Hohenstiel-Schwangau
Saviour of Society

ISBN/EAN: 9783337172602

Printed in Europe, USA, Canada, Australia, Japan

Cover: Foto ©ninafisch / pixelio.de

More available books at **www.hansebooks.com**

PRINCE HOHENSTIEL-SCHWANGAU,

SAVIOUR OF SOCIETY.

BY

ROBERT BROWNING.

SMITH, ELDER AND CO., LONDON.
1871.

"Ὕδραν φονεύσας, μυρίων τ' ἄλλων πόνων
διῆλθον ἀγέλας . . .
τὸ λοίσθιον δὲ τόνδ' ἔτλην τάλας πόνον,
. . . δῶμα θριγκῶσαι κακοῖς.

I slew the Hydra, and from labour pass'd
To labour—tribes of labours ! Till, at last,
Attempting one more labour, in a trice,
Alack, with ills I *crowned the edifice*.

PRINCE HOHENSTIEL-SCHWANGAU,

SAVIOUR OF SOCIETY.

You have seen better days, dear? So have I—

And worse too, for they brought no such bud-mouth

As yours to lisp " You wish you knew me !"   Well,

Wise men, 't is said, have sometimes wished the same,

And wished and had their trouble for their pains.

Suppose my Œdipus should lurk at last

Under a pork-pie hat and crinoline,

And, latish, pounce on Sphynx in Leicester Square?

Or likelier, what if Sphynx in wise old age,

Grown sick of snapping foolish people's heads,

And jealous for her riddle's proper rede,—

Jealous that the good trick which served the turn

Have justice rendered it, nor class one day

With friend Home's stilts and tongs and medium-ware,—

What if the once redoubted Sphynx, I say,

(Because night draws on, and the sands increase,

And desert-whispers grow a prophecy)

Tell all to Corinth of her own accord,

Bright Corinth, not dull Thebes, for Laïs' sake,

Who finds me hardly grey, and likes my nose,

And thinks a man of sixty at the prime?

Good! It shall be! Revealment of myself!

But listen, for we must co-operate ;

I don't drink tea : permit me the cigar !

First, how to make the matter plain, of course—

What was the law by which I lived.   Let 's see :

Ay, we must take one instant of my life

Spent sitting by your side in this neat room :

Watch well the way I use it, and don't laugh !

Here's paper on the table, pen and ink :

Give me the soiled bit—not the pretty rose !

See ! having sat an hour, I'm rested now,

Therefore want work : and spy no better work

For eye and hand and mind that guides them both,

During this instant, than to draw my pen

From blot One—thus—up, up to blot Two—thus—

Which I at last reach, thus, and here's my line

Five inches long and tolerably straight:

Better to draw than leave undrawn, I think,

Fitter to do than let alone, I hold,

Though better, fitter, by but one degree.

Therefore it was that, rather than sit still

Simply, my right-hand drew it while my left

Pulled smooth and pinched the moustache to a point.

Now I permit your plump lips to unpurse:

" So far, one possibly may understand

" Without recourse to witchcraft !" True, my dear.

Thus folks begin with Euclid,—finish, how ?

Trying to square the circle !—at any rate,

Solving abstruser problems than this first

" How find the nearest way 'twixt point and point."

Deal but with moral mathematics so—

Master one merest moment's work of mine,

Even this practising with pen and ink,—

Demonstrate why I rather plied the quill

Than left the space a blank,—you gain a fact,

And God knows what a fact's worth !   So proceed

By inference from just this moral fact

—I don't say, to that plaguy quadrature

" What the whole man meant, whom you wish you knew,"

But, what meant certain things he did of old,

Which puzzled Europe,—why, you 'll find them plain,

This way, not otherwise : I guarantee,

Understand one, you comprehend the rest.

Rays from all round converge to any point :

Study the point then ere you track the rays !

The size o' the circle 's nothing; subdivide

Earth, and earth's smallest grain of mustard-seed,

You count as many parts, small matching large,

If you can use the mind's eye : otherwise,

Material optics, being gross at best,

Prefer the large and leave our mind the small—

And pray how many folks have minds can see?

Certainly you—and somebody in Thrace

Whose name escapes me at the moment.   You—

Lend me your mind then !   Analyse with me

This instance of the line 'twixt blot and blot

I rather chose to draw than leave a blank,

Things else being equal.   You are taught thereby

That 't is my nature, when I am at ease,

Rather than idle out my life too long,

To want to do a thing—to put a thought,

Whether a great thought or a little one,

Into an act, as nearly as may be.

Make what is absolutely new—I can't,

Mar what is made already well enough—

I won't : but turn to best account the thing

That 's half-made—that I can.   Two blots, you saw

I knew how to extend into a line

Symmetric on the sheet they blurred before—

Such little act sufficed, this time, such thought.

Now, we 'll extend rays, widen out the verge,

Describè a larger circle ; leave this first

Clod of an instance we began with, rise

To the complete world many clods effect.

Only continue patient while I throw,

Delver-like, spadeful after spadeful up,

Just as truths come, the subsoil of me, mould

Whence spring my moods : your object,—just to find,

Alike from handlift and from barrow-load,

What salts and silts may constitute the earth—

If it be proper stuff to blow man glass,

Or bake him pottery, bear him oaks or wheat—

What's born of me, in brief; which found, all's known.

If it were genius did the digging-job,

Logic would speedily sift its product smooth

And leave the crude truths bare for poetry ;

But I'm no poet, and am stiff i' the back.

What one spread fails to bring, another may.

In goes the shovel and out comes scoop—as here !

I live to please myself. I recognize

Power passing mine, immeasurable, God—

Above me, whom He made, as heaven beyond

Earth—to use figures which assist our sense.

I know that He is there as I am here,

By the same proof, which seems no proof at all,

It so exceeds familiar forms of proof.

Why " there," not " here " ? Because, when I say " there,"

I treat the feeling with distincter shape

That space exists between us : I,—not He,—

Live, think, do human work here—no machine,

His will moves, but a being by myself,

His, and not He who made me for a work,

Watches my working, judges its effect,

But does not interpose.   He did so once,

And probably will again some time—not now,

Life being the minute of mankind, not God's,

In a certain sense, like time before and time

After man's earthly life, so far as man

Needs apprehend the matter.   Am I clear?

Suppose I bid a courier take to-night

(. . . Once for all, let me talk as if I smoked

Yet in the Residenz, a personage:

I must still represent the thing I was,

Galvanically make dead muscle play,

Or how shall I illustrate muscle's use?)

I could then, last July, bid courier take

Message for me, post-haste, a thousand miles.

I bid him, since I have the right to bid,

And, my part done so far, his part begins;

He starts with due equipment, will and power,

Means he may use, misuse, not use at all,

At his discretion, at his peril too.

I leave him to himself: but, journey done,

I count the minutes, call for the result

In quickness and the courier quality,

Weigh its worth, and then punish or reward

According to proved service; not before.

Meantime, he sleeps through noontide, rides till dawn,

Sticks to the straight road, tries the crooked path,

Measures and manages resource, trusts, doubts

Advisers by the wayside, does his best

At his discretion, lags or launches forth,

(He knows and I know) at his peril too.

You see? Exactly thus men stand to God :

I with my courier, God with me. Just so

I have His bidding to perform ; but mind

And body, all of me, though made and meant

For that sole service, must consult, concert

With my own self and nobody beside,

How to effect the same : God helps not else.

'T is I who, with my stock of craft and strength,

Choose the directer cut across the hedge,

Or keep the foot-track that respects a crop.

Lie down and rest, rise up and run,—live spare,

Feed free,—all that 's my business : but, arrive,

Deliver message, bring the answer back,

And make my bow, I must : then God will speak,

Praise me or haply blame as service proves.

To other men, to each and everyone,

Another law ! what likelier ? God, perchance,

Grants each new man, by some as new a mode,

Intercommunication with Himself,

Wreaking on finiteness infinitude ;

By such a series of effects, gives each

Last His own imprint : old yet ever new

The process : 't is the way of Deity.

How it succeeds, He knows : I only know

That varied modes of creatureship abound,

Implying just as varied intercourse

For each with the creator of them all.

Each has his own mind and no other's mode.

What mode may yours be ？ I shall sympathize !

No doubt, you, good young lady that you are,

Despite a natural naughtiness or two,

Turn eyes up like a Pradier Magdalen

And see an outspread providential hand

Above the owl's-wing aigrette—guard and guide—

Visibly o'er your path, about your bed,

Through all your practisings with London-town.

It points, you go ; it stays fixed, and you stop;

You quicken its procedure by a word

Spoken, a thought in silence, prayer and praise.

Well, I believe that such a hand may stoop,

And such appeals to it may stave off harm,

Pacify the grim guardian of this Square,

And stand you in good stead on quarter-day :

Quite possible in your case ; not in mine.

" Ah, but I choose to make the difference,

Find the emancipation?" No, I hope!

If I deceive myself, take noon for night,

Please to become determinedly blind

To the true ordinance of human life,

Through mere presumption—that is my affair,

And truly a grave one ; but as grave I think

Your affair, yours, the specially observed,—

Each favored person that perceives his path

Pointed him, inch by inch, and looks above

For guidance, through the mazes of this world,

In what we call its meanest life-career

—Not how to manage Europe properly,

But how keep open shop, and yet pay rent,

Rear household, and make both ends meet, the same.

I say, such man is no less tasked than I

To duly take the path appointed him

By whatsoever sign he recognize.

Our insincerity on both our heads !

No matter what the object of a life,

Small work or large,—the making thrive a shop,

Or seeing that an empire take no harm,—

There are known fruits to judge obedience by.

You 've read a ton's weight, now, of newspaper—

Lives of me, gabble about the kind of prince—

You know my work i' the rough ; I ask you, then,

Do I appear subordinated less

To hand-impulsion, one prime push for all,

Than little lives of men, the multitude

That cried out, every quarter of an hour,

For fresh instructions, did or did not work,

And praised in the odd minutes?

Eh, my dear?

Such is the reason why I acquiesced

In doing what seemed best for me to do,

So as to please myself on the great scale,

Having regard to immortality

No less than life— did that which head and heart

Prescribed my hand, in measure with its means

Of doing—used my special stock of power—

Not from the aforesaid head and heart alone,

But every sort of helpful circumstance,

Some problematic and some nondescript:

All regulated by the single care

I' the last resort—that I made thoroughly serve

The when and how, toiled where was need, reposed

As resolutely to the proper point,

Braved sorrow, courted joy, to just one end :

Namely, that just the creature I was bound

To be, I should become, nor thwart at all

God's purpose in creation.   I conceive

No other duty possible to man,—

Highest mind, lowest mind,—no other law

By which to judge life failure or success :

What folks call being saved or cast away.

Such was my rule of life ; I worked my best

Subject to ultimate judgment, God's not man's.

Well then, this settled,—take your tea, I beg,

And meditate the fact, 'twixt sip and sip,—

This settled—why I pleased myself, you saw,

By turning blot and blot into a line,

O' the little scale,—we 'll try now (as your tongue

Tries the concluding sugar-drop) what 's meant

To please me most o' the great scale. Why, just now,

With nothing else to do within my reach,

Did I prefer making two blots one line

To making yet another separate

Third blot, and leaving those I found unlinked?

It meant, I like to use the thing I find,

Rather than strive at unfound novelty:

I make the best of the old, nor try for new.

Such will to act, such choice of action's way,

Constitute—when at work on the great scale,

Driven to their farthest natural consequence

By all the help from all the means—my own

Particular faculty of serving God,

Instinct for putting power to exercise

Upon some wish and want o' the time, I prove

Possible to mankind as best I may.

This constitutes my mission,—grant the phrase,—

Namely, to rule men—men within my reach,

To order, influence and dispose them so

As render solid and stabilify

Mankind in particles, the light and loose,

For their good and my pleasure in the act.

Such good accomplished proves twice good to me—

Good for its own sake, as the just and right,

And, in the effecting also, good again

To me its agent, tasked as suits my taste.

Is this much easy to be understood

At first glance?   Now begin the steady gaze !

My rank—(if I must tell you simple truth—

Telling were else not worth the whiff o' the weed

I lose for the tale's sake)—dear, my rank i' the world

Is hard to know and name precisely : err

I may, but scarcely over-estimate

My style and title.   Do I class with men

Most useful to their fellows?   Possibly,—

Therefore, in some sort, best; but, greatest mind

And rarest nature?   Evidently no.

A conservator, call me, if you please,

Not a creator nor destroyer: one

Who keeps the world safe.   I profess to trace

The broken circle of society,

Dim actual order, I can redescribe

Not only where some segment silver-true

Stays clear, but where the breaks of black commence

Baffling you all who want the eye to probe—

As I make out yon problematic thin

White paring of your thumb-nail outside there,

Above the plaster-monarch on his steed—

See an inch, name an ell, and prophecy

O' the rest that ought to follow, the round moon

Now hiding in the night of things : that round,

I labour to demonstrate moon enough

For the month's purpose,—that society,

Render efficient for the age's need:

Preserving you in either case the old,

Nor aiming at a new and greater thing,

A sun for moon, a future to be made

By first abolishing the present law:

No such proud task for me by any means !

History shows you men whose master-touch

Not so much modifies as makes anew :

Minds that transmute nor need restore at all.

A breath of God made manifest in flesh

Subjects the world to change, from time to time,

Alters the whole conditions of our race

Abruptly, not by unperceived degrees

Nor play of elements already there,

But quite new leaven, leavening the lump,

And liker, so, the natural process.   See!

Where winter reigned for ages—by a turn

I' the time, some star-change, (ask geologists)

The ice-tracts split, clash, splinter and disperse,

And there 's an end of immobility,

Silence, and all that tinted pageant, base

To pinnacle, one flush from fairy-land

Dead-asleep and deserted somewhere,—see!—

As a fresh sun, wave, spring and joy outburst.

Or else the earth it is, time starts from trance,

Her mountains tremble into fire, her plains

Heave blinded by confusion: what result?

New teeming growth, surprises of strange life

Impossible before, a world broke up

And re-made, order gained by law destroyed.

Not otherwise, in our society

Follow like portents, all as absolute

Regenerations : they have birth at rare

Uncertain unexpected intervals

O' the world, by ministry impossible

Before and after fulness of the days :

Some dervish desert-spectre, swordsman, saint,

Law-giver, lyrist,—Oh, we know the names !

Quite other these than I.   Our time requires

No such strange potentate,—who else would dawn,—

No fresh force till the old have spent itself.

Such seems the natural economy.

To shoot a beam into the dark, assists :

To make that beam do fuller service, spread

And utilize such bounty to the height,

That assists also,—and that work is mine.

I recognize, contemplate, and approve

The general compact of society,

Not simply as I see effected good,

But good i' the germ, each chance that 's possible

I' the plan traced so far : all results, in short,

For better or worse of the operation due

To those exceptional natures, unlike mine,

Who, helping, thwarting, conscious, unaware,

Did somehow manage to so far describe

This diagram left ready to my hand,

Waiting my turn of trial.   I see success,

See failure, see what makes or mars throughout.

How shall I else but help complete this plan

Of which I know the purpose and approve,

By letting stay therein what seems to stand,

And adding good thereto of easier reach

To-day than yesterday?

     So much, no more!

Whereon, " No more than that?"—inquire aggrieved

Half of my critics: "nothing new at all?

The old plan saved, instead of a sponged slate

And fresh-drawn figure?"—while, "So much as that?"

Object their fellows of the other faith:

" Leave uneffaced the crazy labyrinth

Of alteration and amendment, lines

Which every dabster felt in duty bound

To signalize his power of pen and ink

By adding to a plan once plain enough ?

Why keep each fool's bequeathment, scratch and blurr

Which overscrawl and underscore the piece—

Nay, strengthen them by touches of your own ?"

Well, that 's my mission, so I serve the world,

Figure as man o' the moment,—in default

Of somebody inspired to strike such change

Into society—from round to square,

The ellipsis to the rhomboid, how you please,

As suits the size and shape o' the world he finds.

But this I can,—and nobody my peer,—

Do the best with the least change possible :

Carry the incompleteness on, a stage,

Make what was crooked straight, and roughness smooth,

And weakness strong : wherein if I succeed,

It will not prove the worst achievement, sure,

In the eyes at least of one man, one I look

Nowise to catch in critic company :

To-wit, the man inspired, the genius' self

Destined to come and change things thoroughly.

He, at least, finds his business simplified,

Distinguishes the done from undone, reads

Plainly what meant and did not mean this time

We live in, and I work on, and transmit

To such successor : he will operate

On good hard substance, not mere shade and shine.

Let all my critics, born to idleness

And impotency, get their good, and have

Their hooting at the giver : I am deaf—

Who find great good in this society,

Great gain, the purchase of great labour.   Touch

The work I may and must, but—reverent

In every fall o' the finger-tip, no doubt.

Perhaps I find all good there 's warrant for

I' the world as yet : nay, to the end of time,—

Since evil never means part company

With mankind, only shift side and change shape.

I find advance i' the main, and notably

The Present an improvement on the Past,

And promise for the Future—which shall prove

Only the Present with its rough made smooth,

Its indistinctness emphasized; I hope

No better, nothing newer for mankind,

But something equably smoothed everywhere,

Good, reconciled with hardly-quite-as-good,

Instead of good and bad each jostling each.

"And that 's all?" Ay, and quite enough for me !

We have toiled so long to gain what gain I find

I' the Present,—let us keep it ! We shall toil

So long before we gain—if gain God grant—

A Future with one touch of difference

I' the heart of things, and not their outside face,—

Let us not risk the whiff of my cigar

For Fourier, Comte and all that ends in smoke !

This I see clearest probably of men

With power to act and influence, now alive :

Juster than they to the true state of things ;

In consequence, more tolerant that, side

By side, shall co-exist and thrive alike

In the age, the various sorts of happiness

Moral, mark !—not material—moods o' the mind

Suited to man and man his opposite :

Say, minor modes of movement—hence to there,

Or thence to here, or simply round about—

So long as each toe spares its neighbour's kibe,

Nor spoils the major march and main advance.

The love of peace, care for the family,

Contentment with what 's bad but might be worse—

Good movements these ! and good, too, discontent,

So long as that spurs good, which might be best,

Into becoming better, anyhow :

Good—pride of country, putting hearth and home

I' the back-ground, out of undue prominence :

Good—yearning after change, strife, victory,

And triumph.   Each shall have its orbit marked,

But no more,—none impede the other's path

In this wide world,—though each and all alike,

Save for me, fain would spread itself through space

And leave its fellow not an inch of way.

I rule and regulate the course, excite,

Restrain : because the whole machine should march

Impelled by those diversely-moving parts,

Each blind to aught beside its little bent.

Out of the turnings round and round inside,

Comes that straight-forward world-advance, I want,

And none of them supposes God wants too

And gets through just their hindrance and my help.

I think that to have held the balance straight

5

For twenty years, say, weighing claim and claim,

And giving each its due, no less no more,

This was good service to humanity,

Right usage of my power in head and heart,

And reasonable piety beside.

Keep those three points in mind while judging me !

You stand, perhaps, for some one man, not men,—

Represent this or the other interest,

Nor mind the general welfare,—so, impugn

My practice and dispute my value : why?

You man of faith, I did not tread the world

Into a paste, and thereof make a smooth

Uniform mound whereon to plant your flag,

The lily-white, above the blood and brains !

Nor yet did I, you man of faithlessness,

So roll things to the level which you love,

That you could stand at ease there and survey

The universal Nothing undisgraced

By pert obtrusion of some old church-spire

I' the distance ! Neither friend would I content,

Nor, as the world were simply meant for him,

Thrust out his fellow and mend God's mistake.

Why, you two fools,—my dear friends all the same,—

Is it some change o' the world and nothing else

Contents you ? Should whatever was, not be ?

How thanklessly you view things ! There 's the root

Of the evil, source of the entire mistake :

You see no worth i' the world, nature and life,

Unless we change what is to what may be,

Which means,—may be, i' the brain of one of you !

" Reject what is ? "—all capabilities—

Nay, you may style them chances if you choose—

All chances, then, of happiness that lie

Open to anybody that is born,

Tumbles into this life and out again,—

All that may happen, good and evil too,

I' the space between, to each adventurer

Upon this 'sixty, Anno Domini :

A life to live—and such a life ! a world

To learn, one's lifetime in,—and such a world !

However did the foolish pass for wise

By calling life a burden, man a fly

Or worm or what 's most insignificant ?

" O littleness of man !" deplores the bard ;

And then, for fear the Powers should punish him,

" O grandeur of the visible universe

Our human littleness contrasts withal !

O sun, O moon, ye mountains and thou sea,

Thou emblem of immensity, thou this,

That and the other,—what impertinence

In man to eat and drink and walk about

And have his little notions of his own,

The while some wave sheds foam upon the shore !"

First of all, 't is a lie some three-times thick :

The bard,—this sort of speech being poetry,—

The bard puts mankind well outside himself

And then begins instructing them : " This way

I and my friend the sea conceive of you !

What would you give to think such thoughts as ours

Of you and the sea together ?" Down they go

On the humbled knees of them : at once they draw

Distinction, recognize no mate of theirs

In one, despite his mock humility,

So plain a match for what he plays with.   Next,

The turn of the great ocean-play-fellow,

When the bard, leaving Bond Street very far

From ear-shot, cares not to ventriloquize,

But tells the sea its home-truths : "You, my match?

You, all this terror and immensity

And what not?   Shall I tell you what you are?

Just fit to hitch into a stanza, so

Wake up and set in motion who 's asleep

O' the other side of you, in England, else

Unaware, as folk pace their Bond Street now,

Somebody here despises them so much !

Between us,—they are the ultimate ! to them

And their perception go these lordly thoughts :

Since what were ocean—mane and tail, to boot—

Mused I not here, how make thoughts thinkable ?

Start forth my stanza and astound the world !

Back, billows, to your insignificance !

Deep, you are done with ! "

       Learn, my gifted friend,

There are two things i' the world, still wiser folk

Accept—intelligence and sympathy.

You pant about unutterable power

I' the ocean, all you feel but cannot speak ?

Why, that 's the plainest speech about it all.

You did not feel what was not to be felt.

Well, then, all else but what man feels is nought—

The wash o' the liquor that o'erbrims the cup

Called man, and runs to waste adown his side,

Perhaps to feed a cataract,—who cares?

I 'll tell you : all the more I know mankind,

The more I thank God, like my grandmother,

For making me a little lower than

The angels, honor-clothed and glory-crowned :

This is the honor,—that no thing I know,

Feel or conceive, but I can make my own

Somehow, by use of hand or head or heart :

This is the glory,—that in all conceived,

Or felt or known, I recognize a mind

Not mine but like mine,—for the double joy,—

Making all things for me and me for Him.

There 's folly for you at this time of day !

So think it ! and enjoy your ignorance

Of what—no matter for the worthy's name—

Wisdom set working in a noble heart,

When he, who was earth's best geometer

Up to that time of day, consigned his life

With its results into one matchless book,

The triumph of the human mind so far,

All in geometry man yet could do :

And then wrote on the dedication-page

In place of name the universe applauds,

' But, God, what a geometer art Thou ! "

I suppose Heaven is, through Eternity,

The equalizing, ever and anon,

In momentary rapture, great with small,

6

Omniscience with intelligency, God

With man,—the thunder-glow from pole to pole

Abolishing, a blissful moment-space,

Great cloud alike and small cloud, in one fire—

As sure to ebb as sure again to flow

When the new receptivity deserves

The new completion.   There 's the Heaven for me.

And I say, therefore, to live out one's life

I' the world here, with the chance,—whether by pain

Or pleasure be the process, long or short

The time, august or mean the circumstance

To human eye,—of learning how set foot

Decidedly on some one path to Heaven,

Touch segment in the circle whence all lines

Lead to the centre equally, red lines

Or black lines, so they but produce themselves—

This, I do say,—and here my sermon ends,—

This makes it worth our while to tenderly

Handle a state of things which mend we might,

Mar we may, but which meanwhile helps so far.

Therefore my end is—save society !

" And that 's all ? " twangs the never-failing taunt

O' the foe—" No novelty, creativeness,

Mark of the master that renews the age ? "

" Nay, all that ? " rather will demur my judge

I look to hear some day, nor friend nor foe—

" Did you attain, then, to perceive that God

Knew what He undertook when He made things ? "

Ay : that my task was to co-operate

Rather than play the rival, chop and change

The order whence comes all the good we know,

With this,—good's last expression to our sense,—

That there 's a further good conceivable

Beyond the utmost earth can realize :

And, therefore, that to change the agency,

The evil whereby good is brought about—

Try to make good do good as evil does—

Were just as if a chemist, wanting white,

And knowing black ingredients bred the dye,

Insisted these too should be white forsooth !

Correct the evil, mitigate your best,

Blend mild with harsh, and soften black to gray

If gray may follow with no detriment

To the eventual perfect purity !

But as for hazarding the main result

By hoping to anticipate one half

In the intermediate process,—no, my friends !

This bad world, I experience and approve ;

Your good world,—with no pity, courage, hope,

Fear, sorrow, joy,—devotedness, in short,

Which I account the ultimate of man,

Of which there 's not one day nor hour but brings,

In flower or fruit, some sample of success,

Out of this same society I save—

None of it for me !   That I might have none,

I rapped your tampering knuckles twenty years.

Such was the task imposed me, such my end.

Now for the means thereto.   Ah, confidence—

Keep we together or part company?

This is the critical minute!   " Such my end?"

Certainly; how could it be otherwise?

Can there be question which was the right task—

To save or to destroy society?

Why, even prove that, by some miracle,

Destruction were the proper work to choose,

And that a torch best remedies what 's wrong

I' the temple, whence the long procession wound

Of powers and beauties, earth's achievements all,

The human strength that strove and overthrew,—

The human love that, weak itself, crowned strength,—

The instinct crying " God is whence I came!"—

The reason laying down the law " And such

His will i' the world must be!"—the leap and shout

Of genius " For I hold His very thoughts,

The meaning of the mind of Him !"—nay, more

The ingenuities, each active force

That turning in a circle on itselt

Looks neither up nor down but keeps the spot,

Mere creature-like and, for religion, works,

Works only and works ever, makes and shapes

And changes, still wrings more of good from less,

Still stamps some bad out, where was worst before,

So leaves the handiwork, the act and deed,

Were it but house and land and wealth, to show

Here was a creature perfect in the kind—

Whether as bee, beaver, or behemoth,

What 's the importance? he has done his work

For work's sake, worked well, earned a creature's praise;—

I say, concede that same fane, whence deploys

Age after age, all this humanity,

Diverse but ever dear, out of the dark

Behind the altar into the broad day

By the portal—enter, and, concede there mocks

Each lover of free motion and much space

A perplexed length of apse and aisle and nave,—

Pillared roof and carved screen, and what care I ?—

That irk the movement and impede the march,—

Nay, possibly, bring flat upon his nose

At some odd break-neck angle, by some freak

Of old-world artistry, that personage

Who, could he but have kept his skirts from grief

And catching at the hooks and crooks about,

Had stepped out on the daylight of our time

Plainly the man of the age,—still, still, I bar

Excessive conflagration in the case.

" Shake the flame freely ! " shout the multitude :

The architect approves I stuck my torch

Inside a good stout lantern, hung its light

Above the hooks and crooks, and ended so.

To save society was well : the means

Whereby to save it,—there begins the doubt

Permitted you, imperative on me ;

Were mine the best means?   Did I work aright

With powers appointed me ?—since powers denied

Concern me nothing.

          Well, my work reviewed

Fairly, leaves more hope than discouragement.

First, there 's the deed done : what I found, I leave,—

What tottered, I kept stable : if it stand

One month, without sustainment, still thank me

The twenty years' sustainer !   Now, observe,

Sustaining is no brilliant self-display

Like knocking down or even setting up :

Much bustle these necessitate ; and still

To vulgar eye, the mightier of the myth

Is Hercules, who substitutes his own

For Atlas' shoulder and supports the globe

A whole day,—not the passive and obscure

Atlas who bore, ere Hercules was born,

And is to go on bearing that same load

When Hercules turns ash on Œta's top.

'T is the transition-stage, the tug and strain,

That strike men : standing still is stupid-like.

My pressure was too constant on the whole

For any part's eruption into space ·

Mid sparkles, crackling, and much praise of me.

I saw that, in the ordinary life,

Many of the little make a mass of men

Important beyond greatness here and there ;

As certainly as, in life exceptional,

When old things terminate and new commence,

A solitary great man 's worth the world.

God takes the business into His own hands

At such time : who creates the novel flower

Contrives to guard and give it breathing-room :

I merely tend the corn-field, care for crop,

And weed no acre thin to let emerge

What prodigy may stifle there perchance,

—No, though my eye have noted where he lurks.

Oh those mute myriads that spoke loud to me—

The eyes that craved to see the light, the mouths

That sought the daily bread and nothing more,

The hands that supplicated exercise,

Men that had wives, and women that had babes,

And all these making suit to only live !

Was I to turn aside from husbandry,

Leave hope of harvest for the corn, my care,

To play at horticulture, rear some rose

Or poppy into perfect leaf and bloom

When, mid the furrows, up was pleased to sprout

Some man, cause, system, special interest

I ought to study, stop the world meanwhile ?

" But I am Liberty, Philanthropy,

Enlightenment, or Patriotism, the power

Whereby you are to stand or fall !" cries each :

" Mine and mine only be the flag you flaunt !"

And, when I venture to object " Meantime,

What of yon myriads with no flag at all—

My crop which, who flaunts flag must tread across ?"

" Now, this it is to have a puny mind !"

Admire my mental prodigies : " down—down—

Ever at home o' the level and the low,

There bides he brooding ! Could he look above,

With less of the owl and more of the eagle eye,

He 'd see there 's no way helps the little cause

Like the attainment of the great.   Dare first

The chief emprise ; dispel yon cloud between

The sun and us ; nor fear that, though our heads

Find earlier warmth and comfort from his ray,

What lies about our feet, the multitude,

Will fail of benefaction presently.

Come now, let each of us awhile cry truce

To special interests, make common cause

Against the adversary—or perchance

Mere dullard to his own plain interest !

Which of us will you choose ?—since needs must be

Some one o' the warring causes you incline

To hold, i' the main, has right and should prevail :

Why not adopt and give it prevalence ?

Choose strict Faith or lax Incredulity,—

King, Caste and Cultus—or the Rights of Man,

Sovereignty of each Proudhon o'er himself,

And all that follows in just consequence !

Go free the stranger from a foreign yoke ;

Or stay, concentrate energy at home ;

Succeed !—when he deserves, the stranger will.

Comply with the Great Nation's impulse, print

By force of arms,—since reason pleads in vain,

And, mid the sweet compulsion, pity weeps,—

Hohenstiel-Schwangau on the universe !

Snub the Great Nation, cure the impulsive itch

With smartest fillip on a restless nose

Was ever launched by thumb and finger !   Bid

Hohenstiel-Schwangau first repeal the tax

On pig-tails and pomatum and then mind

Abstruser matters for next century !

Is your choice made ?   Why then, act up to choice !

Leave the illogical touch now here now there

I' the way of work, the tantalizing help

First to this then the other opposite :

The blowing hot and cold, sham policy,

Sure ague of the mind and nothing more,

Disease of the perception or the will,

That fain would hide in a fine name !   Your choice,

Speak it out and condemn yourself thereby !"

Well, Leicester-square is not the Residenz :

Instead of shrugging shoulder, turning friend

The deaf ear, with a wink to the police—

I 'll answer—by a question, wisdom's mode.

How many years, o' the average, do men

Live in this world ?   Some score, say computists.

Quintuple me that term and give mankind

The likely hundred, and with all my heart

I 'll take your task upon me, work your way,

Concentrate energy on some one cause :

Since, counseller, I also have my cause,

My flag, my faith in its effect, my hope

In its eventual triumph for the good

O' the world.   And once upon a time, when I

Was like all you, mere voice and nothing more,

Myself took wings, soared sun-ward, and thence sang

" Look where I live i' the loft, come up to me,

Groundlings, nor grovel longer ! gain this height,

And prove you breathe here better than below !

Why, what emancipation far and wide

Will follow in a trice ! They too can soar,

Each tenant of the earth's circumference

Claiming to elevate humanity,

They also must attain such altitude,

Live in the luminous circle that surrounds

The planet, not the leaden orb itself.

Press out, each point, from surface to yon verge

Which one has gained and guaranteed your realm !"

Ay, still my fragments wander, music-fraught,

Sighs of the soul, mine once, mine now, and mine

For ever !   Crumbled arch, crushed aqueduct,

Alive with tremors in the shaggy growth

Of wild-wood, crevice-sown, that triumphs there

Imparting exultation to the hills !

Sweep of the swathe when only the winds walk

And waft my words above the grassy sea

Under the blinding blue that basks o'er Rome,—

Hear ye not still—" Be Italy again ?"

And ye, what strikes the panic to your heart ?

Decrepit council-chambers,—where some lamp

Drives the unbroken black three paces off

From where the greybeards huddle in debate,

Dim cowls and capes, and midmost glimmers one

Like tarnished gold, and what they say is doubt,

And what they think is fear, and what suspends

The breath in them is not the plaster-patch

Time disengages from the painted wall

Where Rafael moulderingly bids adieu,

Nor tick of the insect turning tapestry

To dust, which a queen's finger traced of old ;

But some word, resonant, redoubtable,

Of who once felt upon his head a hand

Whereof the head now apprehends his foot.

"Light in Rome, Law in Rome, and Liberty

O' the soul in Rome—the free Church, the free State!

Stamp out the nature that 's best typified

By its embodiment in Peter's Dome,

The scorpion-body with the greedy pair

Of outstretched nippers, either colonnade

Agape for the advance of heads and hearts!"

There 's one cause for you! one and only one,

For I am vocal through the universe,

I' the work-shop, manufactory, exchange

And market-place, sea-port and custom-house

O' the frontier: listen if the echoes die—

"Unfettered commerce! Power to speak and hear,

And print and read!   The universal vote!

Its rights for labour!"   This, with much beside,

I spoke when I was voice and nothing more,

But altogether such an one as you

My censors.   " Voice, and nothing more, indeed ! "

Re-echoes round me : " that 's the censure, there 's

Involved the ruin of you soon or late !

Voice,—when its promise beat the empty air :

And nothing more,—when solid earth 's your stage,

And we desiderate performance, deed

For word, the realizing all you dreamed

In the old days : now, for deed, we find at door

O' the council-chamber posted, mute as mouse,

Hohenstiel-Schwangau, sentry and safeguard

O' the greybeards all a-chuckle, cowl to cape,

Who challenge Judas,—that 's endearment's style,—

To stop their mouths or let escape grimace,

While they keep cursing Italy and him.

The power to speak, hear, print and read is ours?

Ay, we learn where and how, when clapped inside

A convict-transport bound for cool Cayenne!

The universal vote we have: its urn,

We also have where votes drop, fingered-o'er

By the universal Prefect.   Say, Trade 's free

And Toil turned master out o' the slave it was:

What then?   These feed man's stomach, but his soul

Craves finer fare, nor lives by bread alone,

As somebody says somewhere.   Hence you stand

Proved and recorded either false or weak,

Faulty in promise or performance: which?"

Neither, I hope.   Once pedestalled on earth,

To act not speak, I found earth was not air.

I saw that multitude of mine, and not

The nakedness and nullity of air

Fit only for a voice to float in free.

Such eyes I saw that craved the light alone,

Such mouths that wanted bread and nothing else,

Such hands that supplicated handiwork,

Men with the wives, and women with the babes,

Yet all these pleading just to live, not die!

Did I believe one whit less in belief,

Take truth for falsehood, wish the voice revoked

That told the truth to heaven for earth to hear?

No, this should be, and shall; but when and how?

At what expense to these who average

Your twenty years of life, my computists?

" Not bread alone " but bread before all else

For these : the bodily want serve first, said I ;

If earth-space and the life-time help not here,

Where is the good of body having been?

But, helping body, if we somewhat baulk

The soul of finer fare, such food 's to find

Elsewhere and afterward—all indicates,

Even this self-same fact that soul can starve

Yet body still exist its twenty years :

While, stint the body, there 's an end at once

O' the revel in the fancy that Rome 's free,

And superstition 's fettered, and one prints

Whate'er one pleases and who pleases reads

The same, and speaks out and is spoken to,

And divers hundred thousand fools may vote

A vote untampered with by one wise man,

And so elect Barabbas deputy

In lieu of his concurrent.   I who trace

The purpose written on the face of things,

For my behoof and guidance—(whoso needs

No such sustainment, sees beneath my signs,

Proves, what I take for writing, penmanship,

Scribble and flourish with no sense for me

O' the sort I solemnly go spelling out,—

Let him ! there 's certain work of mine to show

Alongside his work : which gives warranty

Of shrewder vision in the workman—judge !)

I who trace Providence without a break

I' the plan of things, drop plumb on this plain print

9

Of an intention with a view to good,

That man is made in sympathy with man '

At outset of existence, so to speak ;

But in dissociation, more and more,

Man from his fellow, as their lives advance

In culture ; still humanity, that's born

A mass, keeps flying off, fining away

Ever into a multitude of points,

And ends in isolation, each from each :

Peerless above i' the sky, the pinnacle,—

Absolute contact, fusion, all below

At the base of being.   How comes this about ?

This stamp of God characterizing man

And nothing else but man in the universe—

That, while he feels with man (to use man's speech)

I' the little things of life, its fleshly wants

Of food and rest and health and happiness,

Its simplest spirit-motions, loves and hates,

Hopes, fears, soul-cravings on the ignoblest scale,

O' the fellow-creature,—owns the bond at base,—

He tends to freedom and divergency

In the upward progress, plays the pinnacle

When life 's at greatest (grant again the phrase !

Because there 's neither great nor small in life.)

" Consult thou for thy kind that have the eyes

To see, the mouths to eat, the hands to work,

Men with the wives, and women with the babes !"

Prompts Nature. " Care thou for thyself alone

I' the conduct of the mind God made thee with !

Think, as if man had never thought before !

Act, as if all creation hung attent

On the acting of such faculty as thine,

To take prime pattern from thy masterpiece !"

Nature prompts also : neither law obeyed

To the uttermost 'by any heart and soul

We know or have in record : both of them

Acknowledged blindly by whatever man

We ever knew or heard of in this world.

" Will you have why and wherefore, and the fact

Made plain as pikestaff ?" modern Science asks.

" That mass man sprung from was a jelly-lump

Once on a time ; he kept an after course

Through fish and insect, reptile, bird and beast,

Till he attained to be an ape at last

Or last but one.   And if this doctrine shock

In aught the natural pride " . . . . Friend, banish fear,

The natural humility replies !

Do you suppose, even I, poor potentate,

Hohenstiel-Schwangau, who once ruled the roast,—

I was born able at all points to ply

My tools ? or did I have to learn my trade,

Practise as exile ere perform as prince ?

The world knows something of my ups and downs :

But grant me time, give me the management

And manufacture of a model me,

Me fifty-fold, a prince without a flaw,—

Why, there 's no social grade, the sordidest,

My embryo potentate should blink and scape.

King, all the better he was cobbler once,

He should know, sitting on the throne, how tastes

Life to who sweeps the doorway.   But life 's hard,

Occasion rare; you cut probation short,

And, being half-instructed, on the stage

You shuffle through your part as best you may,

And bless your stars, as I do.   God takes time.

I like the thought He should have lodged me once

I' the hole, the cave, the hut, the tenement,

The mansion and the palace ; made me learn

The feel o' the first, before I found myself

Loftier i' the last, not more emancipate ;

From first to last of lodging, I was I,

And not at all the place that harboured me.

Do I refuse to follow farther yet

I' the backwardness, repine if tree and flower,

Mountain or streamlet were my dwelling-place

Before I gained enlargement, grew mollusc?

As well account that way for many a thrill

Of kinship, I confess to, with the powers

Called Nature : animate, inanimate,

In parts or in the whole, there 's something there

Man-like that somehow meets the man in me.

My pulse goes altogether with the heart

O' the Persian, that old Xerxes, when he stayed

His march to conquest of the world, a day

I' the desert, for the sake of one superb

Plane-tree which queened it there in solitude :

Giving her neck its necklace, and each arm

Its armlet, suiting soft waist, snowy side,

With cincture and apparel.   Yes, I lodged

In those successive tenements ; perchance

Taste yet the straitness of them while I stretch

Limb and enjoy new liberty the more.

And some abodes are lost or ruinous;

Some, patched-up and pieced out, and so transformed

They still accommodate the traveller

His day of life-time.   O you count the links,

Descry no bar of the unbroken man ?

Yes,—and who welds a lump of ore, suppose

He likes to make a chain and not a bar,

And reach by link on link, link small, link large,

Out to the due length—why, there 's forethought still

Outside o' the series, forging at one end,

While at the other there 's—no matter what

The kind of critical intelligence

Believing that last link had last but one

For parent, and no link was, first of all,

Fitted to anvil, hammered into shape.

Else, I accept the doctrine, and deduce

This duty, that I recognize mankind,

In all its height and depth and length and breadth.

Mankind i' the main have little wants, not large:

I, being of will and power to help, i' the main,

Mankind, must help the least wants first. My friend,

That is, my foe, without such power and will,

May plausibly concentrate all he wields,

And do his best at helping some large want,

Exceptionally noble cause, that 's seen

Subordinate enough from where I stand.

As he helps, I helped once, when like himself,

Unable to help better, work more wide;

And so would work with heart and hand to-day,

Did only computists confess a fault,

And multiply the single score by five,

Five only, give man's life its hundred years.

Change life, in me shall follow change to match !

Time were then, to work here, there, everywhere,

By turns and try experiment at ease !

Full time to mend as well as mar : why wait

The slow and sober uprise all around

O' the building ?   Let us run up, right to roof,

Some sudden marvel, piece of perfectness,

And testify what we intend the whole !

Is the world losing patience ?   " Wait ! " say we :

" There's time : no generation needs to die

Unsolaced ; you 've a century in store ! "

But, no : I sadly let the voices wing

Their way i' the upper vacancy, nor test

Truth on this solid as I promised once.

Well, and what is there to be sad about ?

The world 's the world, life 's life, and nothing else.

'T is part of life, a property to prize,

That those o' the higher sort engaged i' the world,

Should fancy they can change its ill to good,

Wrong to right, ugliness to beauty : find

Enough success in fancy turning fact,

To keep the sanguine kind in countenance

And justify the hope that busies them :

Failure enough,—to who can follow change

Beyond their vision, see new good prove ill

I' the consequence, see blacks and whites of life

Shift square indeed, but leave the chequered face

Unchanged i' the main,—failure enough for such,

To bid ambition keep the whole from change,

As their best service.   I hope nought beside.

No, my brave thinkers, whom I recognize,

Gladly, myself the first, as, in a sense,

All that our world 's worth, flower and fruit of man !

Such minds myself award supremacy

Over the common insignificance,

When only Mind 's in question,—Body bows

To quite another government, you know.

Be Kant crowned king o' the castle in the air !

Hans Slouch,—his own, and children's mouths to feed

I' the hovel on the ground,—wants meat, nor chews

" The Pure Critique of Reason " in exchange.

But, now,—suppose I could allow your claims

And quite change life to please you,—would it please?

Would life comport with change and still be life?

Ask, now, a doctor for a remedy:

There 's his prescription.   Bid him point you out

Which of the five or six ingredients saves

The sick man.   " Such the efficacity?

Then why not dare and do things in one dose

Simple and pure, all virtue, no alloy

Of the idle drop and powder?"   What 's his word?

The efficacity, neat, were neutralized:

It wants dispersing and retarding,—nay

Is put upon its mettle, plays its part

Precisely through such hindrance everywhere,

Finds some mysterious give and take i' the case,

Some gain by opposition, he foregoes

Should he unfetter the medicament.

So with this thought of yours that fain would work

Free in the world: it wants just what it finds—

The ignorance, stupidity, the hate,

Envy and malice and uncharitableness

That bar your passage, break the flow of you

Down from those happy heights where many a cloud

Combined to give you birth and bid you be

The royalest of rivers : on you glide

Silverly till you reach the summit-edge,

Then over, on to all that ignorance,

Stupidity, hate, envy, bluffs and blocks,

Posted to fret you into foam and noise.

What of it?   Up you mount in minute mist,

And bridge the chasm that crushed your quietude,

A spirit-rainbow, earthborn jewelry

Outsparkling the insipid firmament

Blue above Terni and its orange-trees.

Do not mistake me !   You, too, have your rights !

Hans must not burn Kant's house above his head,

Because he cannot understand Kant's book :

And still less must Hans' pastor burn Kant's self

Because Kant understands some books too well.

But, justice seen to on this little point,

Answer me, is it manly, is it sage

To stop and struggle with arrangements here

It took so many lives, so much of toil,

To tinker up into efficiency ?

Can't you contrive to operate at once,—

Since time is short and art is long,—to show

Your quality i' the world, whate'er you boast,

Without this fractious call on folks to crush

The world together just to set you free,

Admire the capers you will cut perchance,

Nor mind the mischief to your neighbours ?

                                        " Age !

Age and experience bring discouragement,"

You taunt me : I maintain the opposite.

Am I discouraged who,—perceiving health,

Strength, beauty, as they tempt the eye of soul,

Are uncombinable with flesh and blood,—

Resolve to let my body live its best,

And leave my soul what better yet may be

Or not be, in this life or afterward?

—In either fortune, wiser than who waits

Till magic art procure a miracle.

In virtue of my very confidence

Mankind ought to outgrow its babyhood,

I prescribe rocking, deprecate rough hands,

While thus the cradle holds it past mistake.

Indeed, my task 's the harder—equable

Sustainment everywhere, all strain, no push—

Whereby friends credit me with indolence,

Apathy, hesitation. " Stand stock-still

If able to move briskly? ' All a-strain '—

So must we compliment your passiveness?

Sound asleep, rather !"

Just the judgment passed

Upon a statue, luckless like myself,

I saw at Rome once ! 'T was some artist's whim

To cover all the accessories close

I' the group, and leave you only Laocoön

With neither sons nor serpents to denote

The purpose of his gesture.   Then a crowd

Was called to try the question, criticize

Wherefore such energy of legs and arms,

Nay, eyeballs, starting from the socket.   One—

I give him leave to write my history—

Only one said "I think the gesture strives

Against some obstacle we cannot see."

All the rest made their minds up.   " 'T is a yawn

Of sheer fatigue subsiding to repose :

The statue 's ' Somnolency ' clear enough ! "

/

There, my arch stranger-friend, my audience both

And arbitress, you have one half your wish,

At least : you know the thing I tried to do !

All, so far, to my praise and glory—all

Told as befits the self-apologist,—

Who ever promises a candid sweep

And clearance of those errors miscalled crimes

None knows more, none laments so much as he,

And ever rises from confession, proved

A god whose fault was—trying to be man.

Just so, fair judge,—if I read smile aright—

I condescend to figure in your eyes

As biggest heart and best of Europe's friends,

And hence my failure.   God will estimate

Success one day ; and, in the mean time—you !

I daresay there's some fancy of the sort

Frolicking round this final puff I send

To die up yonder in the ceiling-rose,—

Some consolation-stakes, we losers win !

A plague of the return to " I—I—I

Did this, meant that, hoped, feared the other thing ! "

Autobiography, adieu !   The rest

Shall make amends, be pure blame, history

And falsehood : not the ineffective truth,

But Thiers-and-Victor-Hugo exercise.

Hear what I never was, but might have been

I' the better world where goes tobacco-smoke !

Here lie the dozen volumes of my life :

(Did I say " lie?" the pregnant word will serve.)

Cut on to the concluding chapter, though !

Because the little hours begin to strike.

Hurry Thiers-Hugo to the labour's end !

Something like this the unwritten chapter reads.

Exemplify the situation thus !

Hohenstiel-Schwangau, being, no dispute,

Absolute mistress, chose the Assembly, first,

To serve her : chose this man, its President

Afterward, to serve also,—specially

To see that they did service one and all.

And now the proper term of years was out,

When the Head-servant must vacate his place:

And nothing lay so patent to the world

As that his fellow-servants one and all

Were—mildly make we mention—knaves or fools,

Each of them with his purpose flourished full

I' the face of you by word and impudence,

Or filtered slyly out by nod and wink

And nudge upon your sympathetic rib—

That not one minute more did knave or fool

Mean to keep faith and serve as he had sworn

Hohenstiel-Schwangau, once that Head away.

Why did such swear except to get the chance,

When time should ripen and confusion bloom,

Of putting Hohenstielers-Schwangauese

To the true use of human property?

Restoring souls and bodies, this to Pope,

And that to King, that other to his planned

Perfection of a Share-and-share-alike,

That other still, to Empire absolute

In shape of the Head-servant's very self

Transformed to master whole and sole : each scheme

Discussible, concede one circumstance—

That each scheme's parent were, beside himself,

Hohenstiel-Schwangau, not her serving-man

Sworn to do service in the way she chose

Rather than his way : way superlative,

Only,—by some infatuation,—his

And his and his and everyone's but hers

Who stuck to just the Assembly and the Head.

I make no doubt the Head, too, had his dream

Of doing sudden duty swift and sure

On all that heap of untrustworthiness--

Catching each vaunter of the villany

He meant to perpetrate when time was ripe,

Once the Head-servant fairly out of doors,—

And, caging here a knave and there a fool,

Cry " Mistress of the servants, these and me,

Hohenstiel-Schwangau ! I, their trusty Head,

Pounce on a pretty scheme concocting here

That 's stopped, extinguished by my vigilance.

Your property is safe again : but mark !

Safe in these hands, not yours, who lavish trust

Too lightly.   Leave my hands their charge awhile !

I know your business better than yourself :

Let me alone about it ! Some fine day,

Once we are rid of the embarrassment,

You shall look up and see your longings crowned !"

Such fancy may have tempted to be false,

But this man chose truth and was wiser so.

He recognized that for great minds i' the world

There is no trial like the appropriate one

Of leaving little minds their liberty

Of littleness to blunder on through life,

Now, aiming at right end by foolish means,

Now, at absurd achievement through the aid

Of good and wise means : trial to acquiesce

In folly's life-long privilege—though with power

To do the little minds the good they need,

Despite themselves, by just abolishing

Their right to play the part and fill the place

I' the scheme of things He schemed who made alike

Great minds and little minds, saw use for each.

Could the orb sweep those puny particles

It just half-lights at distance, hardly leads

I' the leash—sweep out each speck of them from space

They anticize in with their days and nights

And whirlings round and dancings off, forsooth,

And all that fruitless individual life

One cannot lend a beam to but they spoil—

Sweep them into itself and so, one star,

Preponderate henceforth i' the heritage

Of heaven!   No! in less senatorial phrase,

The man endured to help, not save outright

The multitude by substituting him

For them, his knowledge, will and way, for God's :

Not change the world, such as it is, and was

And will be, for some other, suiting all

Except the purpose of the maker.   No !

He saw that weakness, wickedness will be,

And therefore should be : that the perfect man

As we account perfection—at most pure

O' the special gold, whate'er the form it take,

Head-work or heart-work, fined and thrice-refined

I' the crucible of life, whereto the powers

Of the refiner, one and all, were flung

To feed the flame their utmost,—e'en that block,

He holds out breathlessly triumphant,—breaks

Into some poisonous ore, its opposite,

At the very purest, so compensating

The Adversary—what if we believe ?

For earlier stern exclusion of his stuff.

See the sage, with the hunger for the truth,

And see his system that 's all true, except

The one weak place that 's stanchioned by a lie !

The moralist, that walks with head erect

I' the crystal clarity of air so long,

Until a stumble, and the man 's one mire !

Philanthropy undoes the social knot

With axe-edge, makes love room 'twixt head and trunk !

Religion—but, enough, the thing 's too clear !

Well, if these sparks break out i' the greenest tree,

Our topmost of performance, yours and mine,

What will be done i' the dry ineptitude

Of ordinary mankind, bark and bole,

All seems ashamed of but their mother-earth ?

Therefore throughout his term of servitude

He did the appointed service, and forbore

Extraneous action that were duty else,

Done by some other servant, idle now

Or mischievous : no matter, each his own—

Own task, and, in the end, own praise or blame !

He suffered them strut, prate and brag their best,

Squabble at odds on every point save one,

And there shake hands,—agree to trifle time,

Obstruct advance with, each, his cricket-cry

" Wait till the Head be off the shoulders here !

Then comes my King, my Pope, my Autocrat,

My Socialist Republic to her own—

To-wit, that property of only me,

Hohenstiel-Schwangau who conceits herself

Free, forsooth, and expects I keep her so !"

—Nay, suffered when, perceiving with dismay

His silence paid no tribute to their noise,

They turned on him. " Dumb menace in that mouth,

Malice in that unstridulosity !

He cannot but intend some stroke of state

Shall signalize his passage into peace

Out of the creaking,—hinder transference

O' the Hohenstielers-Schwangauese to king,

Pope, autocrat, or socialist republic ! That 's

Exact the cause his lips unlocked would cry !

Therefore be stirring : brave, beard, bully him !

Dock, by the million, of its friendly joints,

The electoral body short at once ! who did,

May do again, and undo us beside.

Wrest from his hands the sword for self-defence,

The right to parry any thrust in play

We peradventure please to meditate ! ''

And so forth ; creak, creak, creak : and ne'er a line

His locked mouth oped the wider, till at last

O' the long degraded and insulting day,

Sudden the clock told it was judgment-time.

Then he addressed himself to speak indeed

To the fools, not knaves: they saw him walk straight down

Each step of the eminence, as he first engaged,

And stand at last o' the level,—all he swore.

" People, and not the people's varletry,

This is the task you set myself and these !

Thus I performed my part of it, and thus

They thwarted me throughout, here, here, and here :

Study each instance! yours the loss, not mine.

What they intend now is demonstrable

As plainly: here 's such man, and here 's such mode

Of making you some other than the thing

You, wisely or unwisely, choose to be,

And only set him up to keep you so.

Do you approve this?   Yours the loss, not mine.

Do you condemn it?   There 's a remedy.

Take me—who know your mind, and mean your good,

With clearer head and stouter arm than they,

Or you, or haply anybody else—

And make me master for the moment!   Choose

What time, what power you trust me with : I too

Will choose as frankly ere I trust myself

With time and power : they must be adequate

To the end and aim, since mine the loss, with yours,

If means be wanting; once their worth approved,

Grant them, and I shall forthwith operate—

Ponder it well !—to the extremest stretch

O' the power you trust me: if with unsuccess,

God wills it, and there 's nobody to blame."

Whereon the people answered with a shout

" The trusty one ! no tricksters any more ! "

How could they other?   He was in his place.

What followed?   Just what he foresaw, what proved

The soundness of both judgments,—his, o' the knaves

And fools, each trickster with his dupe,—and theirs,

The people, in what head and arm should help. .

There was uprising, masks dropped, flags unfurled,

Weapons outflourished in the wind, my faith !

Heavily did he let his fist fall plumb

On each perturber of the public peace,

No matter whose the wagging head it broke—

From bald-pate craft and greed and impudence

Of night-hawk at first chance to prowl and prey

For glory and a little gain beside, ·

Passing for eagle in the dusk of the age,—

To florid head-top, foamy patriotism

And tribunitial daring, breast laid bare

Thro' confidence in rectitude, with hand

On private pistol in the pocket : these

And all the dupes of these, who lent themselves

As dust and feather do, to help offence

O' the wind that whirls them at you, then subsides

In safety somewhere, leaving filth afloat,

Annoyance you may brush from eyes and beard,—

These he stopped : bade the wind's spite howl or whine

Its worst outside the building, wind conceives

Meant to be pulled together and become

Its natural playground so.   What foolishness

Of dust or feather proved importunate

And fell 'twixt thumb and finger, found them gripe

To detriment of bulk and buoyancy.

Then followed silence and submission.   Next,

The inevitable comment came on work

And work's cost : he was censured as profuse

Of human life and liberty : too swift

And thorough his procedure, who had lagged

At the outset, lost the opportunity

Through timid scruples as to right and wrong.

" There 's no such certain mark of a small mind "

(So did Sagacity explain the fault)

" As when it needs must square away and sink

To its own small dimensions, private scale

Of right and wrong,—humanity i' the large,

The right and wrong of the universe, forsooth !

This man addressed himself to guard and guide

Hohenstiel-Schwangau.   When the case demands

He frustrate villany in the egg, unhatched,

With easy stamp and minimum of pang

E'en to the punished reptile, ' There's my oath

Restrains my foot,' objects our guide and guard,

' I must leave guardianship and guidance now :

Rather than stretch one handbreadth of the law,

I am bound to see it break from end to end.

First show me death i' the body politic:

Then prescribe pill and potion, what may please

Hohenstiel-Schwangau ! all is for her sake :

'T was she ordained my service should be so.

What if the event demonstrate her unwise,

If she unwill the thing she willed before ?

I hold to the letter and obey the bond

And leave her to perdition loyally.'

Whence followed thrice the expenditure we blame

Of human life and liberty : for want

O' the by-blow, came deliberate butcher's-work ! "

" Elsewhere go carry your complaint ! " bade he.

" Least, largest, there 's one law for all the minds,

Here or above : be true at any price !

'T is just o' the great scale, that such happy stroke

Of falsehood would be found a failure.   Truth

Still stands unshaken at her base by me,

Reigns paramount i' the world, for the large good

O' the long late generations,—I and you   .

Forgotten like this buried foolishness !

Not so the good I rooted in its grave."

This is why he refused to break his oath,

Rather appealed to the people, gained the power

To act as he thought best, then used it, once

For all, no matter what the consequence

To knaves and fools.   As thus began his sway,

So, through its twenty years, one rule of right

Sufficed him : govern for the many first,

The poor mean multitude, all mouths and eyes :

Bid the few, better favoured in the brain,

Be patient, nor presume on privilege,

Help him, or else be quiet,—never crave

That he help them,—increase, forsooth, the gulf

Yawning so terribly 'twixt mind and mind

I' the world here, which his purpose was to block

At bottom, were it by an inch, and bridge,

If by a filament, no more, at top.

Equalize things a little !   And the way

He took to work that purpose out, was plain

Enough to intellect and honesty

And—superstition, style it if you please,

So long as you allow there was no lack

O' the quality imperative in man—

Reverence.   You see deeper? thus saw he,

And by the light he saw, must walk : how else

Was he to do his part? the man's, with might

And main, and not a faintest touch of fear,

Sure he was in the hand of God who comes

Before and after, with a work to do

Which no man helps nor hinders.   Thus the man,—

So timid when the business was to touch

The uncertain order of humanity,

Imperil, for a problematic cure

Of grievance on the surface, any good

I' the deep of things, dim yet discernible —

This same man, so irresolute before,

Show him a true excrescence to cut sheer,

A devil's-graft on God's foundation-stone,

Then—no complaint of indecision more !

He wrenched out the whole canker, root and branch,

Deaf to who cried the world would tumble in

At its four corners if he touched a twig.

Witness that lie of lies, arch-infamy,

When the Republic, with all life involved

In just this law—" Each people rules itself

Its own way, not as any stranger please "—

Turned, and for first proof she was living, bade

Hohenstiel-Schwangau fasten on the throat

Of the first neighbour that claimed benefit

O' the law herself established : " Hohenstiel

For Hohenstielers ! Rome, by parity

Of reasoning, for Romans ? That 's a jest

Wants proper treatment,—lancet-puncture suits

The proud flesh : Rome ape Hohenstiel forsooth ! "

And so the siege and slaughter and success

Whereof we nothing doubt that Hohenstiel

Will have to pay the price, in God's good time,

Which does not always fall on Saturday

When the world looks for wages.   Any how,

He found this infamy triumphant.   Well,—

Sagacity suggested, make this speech !

" The work was none of mine : suppose wrong wait,

Stand over for redressing ?   Mine for me,

My predecessors' work on their own head!

Meantime, there 's plain advantage, should we leave

Things as we find them.   Keep Rome manacled

Hand and foot : no fear of unruliness !

Her foes consent to even seem our friends

So long, no longer.   Then, there 's glory got

I' the boldness and bravado to the world.

The disconcerted world must grin and bear

The old saucy writing,—'Grunt thereat who may,

So shall things be, for such my pleasure is—

Hohenstiel-Schwangau.'   How that reads in Rome

I' the Capitol where Brennus broke his pate !

And what a flourish for our journalists !"

Only, it was nor read nor flourished of,

Since, not a moment did such glory stay

Excision of the canker !   Out it came,

Root and branch, with much roaring, and some blood,

And plentiful abuse of him from friend

And foe.   Who cared ?   Not Nature, that assuaged

The pain and set the patient on his legs

Promptly : the better ! had it been the worse,

'T is Nature you must try conclusions with,

Not he, since nursing canker kills the sick

For certain, while to cut may cure, at least.

" Ah," groaned a second time Sagacity,

" Again the little mind, precipitate,

Rash, rude, when even in the right, as here !

The great mind knows the power of gentleness,

Only tries force because persuasion fails.

Had this man, by prelusive trumpet-blast,

Signified ' Truth and Justice mean to come,

Nay, fast approach your threshold ! Ere they knock,

See that the house be set in order, swept

And garnished, windows shut, and doors thrown wide !

The free State comes to visit the free Church :

Receive her ! or . . or . . never mind what else ! '

Thus moral suasion heralding brute force,

How had he seen the old abuses die,

And new life kindle here, there, everywhere,

Roused simply by that mild yet potent spell—

Beyond or beat of drum or stroke of sword

Public opinion ! "

        " How, indeed ? " he asked,

" When all to see, after some twenty years,

Were your own fool-face waiting for the sight,

Faced by as wide a grin from ear to ear

O' the knaves that, while the fools were waiting, worked—

Broke yet another generation's heart—

Twenty years' respite helping !   Teach your nurse

' Compliance with, before you suck, the teat !'

Find what that means, and meanwhile hold your tongue!"

Whereof the war came which he knew must be.

Now, this had proved the dry-rot of the race

He ruled o'er, that, in the old day, when was need

They fought for their own liberty and life,

Well did they fight, none better: whence, such love

Of fighting somehow still for fighting's sake

Against no matter whose the liberty

And life, so long as self-conceit should crow

And clap the wing, while justice sheathed her claw,—

That what had been the glory of the world

When thereby came the world's good, grew its plague

Now that the champion-armour, donned to dare

The dragon once, was clattered up and down

Highway and by-path of the world at peace,

Merely to mask marauding, or for sake

O' the shine and rattle that apprized the fields

Hohenstiel-Schwangau was a fighter yet,

And would be, till the weary world suppressed

A peccant humour out of fashion now.

Accordingly the world spoke plain at last,

Promised to punish who next played with arms.

So, at his advent, such discomfiture

Taking its true shape of beneficence,

Hohenstiel-Schwangau, half-sad and part-wise,

Sat : if with wistful eye reverting oft

To each pet weapon rusty on its peg,

Yet, with a sigh of satisfaction too

That, peacefulness become the law, herself

Got the due share of godsends in its train,

Cried shame and took advantage quietly.

Still, so the dry-rot had been nursed into

Blood, bones and marrow, that, from worst to best,

All,—clearest brains and soundest hearts, save here,—

All had this lie acceptable for law

Plain as the sun at noonday—" War is best,

Peace is worst; peace we only tolerate

As needful preparation for new war :

War may be for whatever end we will—

Peace only as the proper help thereto.

Such is the law of right and wrong for us

Hohenstiel-Schwangau : for the other world,

As naturally, quite another law.

Are we content?   The world is satisfied.

Discontent ?   Then the world must give us leave

Strike right and left to exercise our arm

Torpid of late through overmuch repose,

And show its strength is still superlative

At somebody 's expense in life or limb :

Which done,—let peace succeed and last a year ! ''

Such devil's-doctrine was so judged God's law,

We say, when this man stepped upon the stage,

That it had seemed a venial fault at most

Had he once more obeyed Sagacity.

" You come i' the happy interval of peace,

The favourable weariness from war :

Prolong it !—artfully, as if intent

On ending peace as soon as possible.

Quietly so increase the sweets of ease

And safety, so employ the multitude,

Put hod and trowel so in idle hands,

So stuff and stop the wagging jaws with bread,

That selfishness shall surreptitiously

Do wisdom's office, whisper in the ear

Of Hohenstiel-Schwangau, there 's a pleasant feel

In being gently forced down, pinioned fast

To the easy arm-chair by the pleading arms

O' the world beseeching her to there abide

Content with all the harm done hitherto,

And let herself be petted in return,

Free to re-wage, in speech and prose and verse,

The old unjust wars, nay—in verse and prose

And speech,—to vaunt new victories, as vile

A plague o' the future,—so that words suffice

For present comfort, and no deeds denote

That,—tired of illimitable line on line

Of boulevard-building, tired o' the theatre

With the tuneful thousand in their thrones above,

For glory of the male intelligence,

And Nakedness in her due niche below,

For illustration of the female use—

She, 'twixt a yawn and sigh, prepares to slip

Out of the arm-chair, wants some blood again

From over the boundary, to colour-up

The sheeny sameness, keep the world aware,

Hohenstiel-Schwangau must have exercise

Despite the petting of the universe !

Come, you're a city-builder : what 's the way

Wisdom takes when time needs that she entice

Some fierce tribe, castled on the mountain-peak,

Into the quiet and amenity

O' the meadow-land below ?   By crying 'Done

With fight now, down with fortress ?'   Rather—'Dare

On, dare ever, not a stone displaced ! '

Cries Wisdom, ' Cradle of our ancestors,

Be bulwark, give our children safety still !

Who of our children please, may stoop and taste

O' the valley-fatness, unafraid,—for why?

At first alarm, they have thy mother-ribs

To run upon for refuge ; foes forget

Scarcely what Terror on her vantage-coigne,

Couchant supreme among the powers of air,

Watches—prepared to pounce—the country wide !'

Meanwhile the encouraged valley holds its own,

From the first hut's adventure in descent,

Half home, half hiding place,—to dome and spire

Befitting the assured metropolis :

Nor means offence to the fort which caps the crag,

All undismantled of a turret-stone,

And bears the banner-pole that creaks at times

Embarrassed by the old emblazonment,

When festal days are to commemorate.

Otherwise left untenanted, no doubt,

Since, never fear, our myriads from below

Would rush, if needs were, man the walls once more,

Renew the exploits of the earlier time

At moment's notice !   But till notice sound,

Inhabit we in ease and opulence ! '

And so, till one day thus a notice sounds,

Not trumpeted, but in a whisper-gust

Fitfully playing through mute city streets

At midnight weary of day's feast and game—

' Friends, your famed fort 's a ruin past repair !

Its use is—to proclaim it had a use

Stolen away long since.   Climb to study there

How to paint barbican and battlement

I' the scenes of our new theatre !   We fight

Now—by forbidding neighbours to sell steel

Or buy wine, not by blowing out their brains !

Moreover, while we let time sap the strength

O' the walls omnipotent in menace once,

Neighbours would seem to have prepared surprise—

Run up defences in a mushroom-growth,

For all the world like what we boasted: brief—

Hohenstiel-Schwangau's policy is peace!'"

Ay, so Sagacity advised him filch

Folly from fools: handsomely substitute

The dagger o' lath, while gay they sang and danced

For that long dangerous sword they liked to feel,

Even at feast-time, clink and make friends start.

No! he said "Hear the truth, and bear the truth,

And bring the truth to bear on all you are

And do, assured that only good comes thence

Whate'er the shape good take! While I have rule,

Understand !—war for war's sake, war for the sake

O' the good war gets you as war's sole excuse,

Is damnable and damned shall be.   You want

Glory ?   Why so do I, and so does God.

Where is it found,—in this paraded shame,—

One particle of glory ?   Once you warred

For liberty against the world, and won :

There was the glory.   Now, you fain would war

Because the neighbour prospers overmuch,—

Because there has been silence half-an-hour,

Like Heaven on earth, without a cannon-shot

Announcing Hohenstielers-Schwangauese

Are minded to disturb the jubilee,—

Because the loud tradition echoes faint,

And who knows but posterity may doubt

If the great deeds were ever done at all,

Much less believe, were such to do again,

So the event would follow : therefore, prove

The old power, at the expense of somebody !

Oh, Glory,—gilded bubble, bard and sage

So nickname rightly,—would thy dance endure

One moment, would thy mocking make believe

Only one upturned eye thy ball was gold,

Had'st thou less breath to buoy thy vacancy

Than a whole multitude expends in praise,

Less range for roaming than from head to head

Of a whole people ? Flit, fall, fly again,

Only, fix never where the resolute hand

May prick thee, prove the lie thou art, at once !

Give me real intellect to reason with,

No multitude, no entity that apes

One wise man, being but a million fools !

How and whence wishest glory, thou wise one?

Would'st get it,—did'st thyself guide Providence,—

By stinting of his due each neighbour round

In strength and knowledge and dexterity

So as to have thy littleness grow large

By all those somethings, once, turned nothings, now,

As children make a molehill mountainous

By scooping out the plain into a trench

And saving so their favourite from approach?

Quite otherwise the cheery game of life,

True yet mimetic warfare, whereby man

Does his best with his utmost, and so ends

The victor most of all in fair defeat.

Who thinks,—would he have no one think beside?

Who knows, who does,—must other learning die

And action perish? Why, our giant proves

No better than a dwarf, with rivalry

Prostrate around him. 'Let the whole race stand

And try conclusions fairly!' he cries first.

Show me the great man would engage his peer

Rather by grinning 'Cheat, thy gold is brass!'

Than granting 'Perfect piece of purest ore!

Still, is it less good mintage, this of mine?'

Well, and these right and sound results of soul

I' the strong and healthy one wise man,—shall such

Be vainly sought for, scornfully renounced

I' the multitude that make the entity—

The people?—to what purpose, if no less,

In power and purity of soul, below

The reach of the unit than, in multiplied

Might of the body, vulgarized the more,

Above, in thick and threefold brutishness?

See ! you accept such one wise man, myself :

Wiser or less wise, still I operate

From my own stock of wisdom, nor exact

Of other sort of natures you admire,

That whoso rhymes a sonnet pays a tax,

Who paints a landscape dips brush at his cost,

Who scores a septett true for strings and wind

Mulcted must be—else how should I impose

Properly, attitudinize aright,

Did such conflicting claims as these divert

Hohenstiel-Schwangau from observing me?

Therefore, what I find facile, you be sure,

With effort or without it, you shall dare—

You, I aspire to make my better self

And truly the Great Nation.   No more war

For war's sake, then ! and,—seeing, wickedness

Springs out of folly,—no more foolish dread

O' the neighbour waxing too inordinate

A rival, through his gain of wealth and ease!

What?—keep me patient, Powers !—the people here,

Earth presses to her heart, nor owns a pride

Above her pride i' the race all flame and air

And aspiration to the boundless Great,

The incommensurably Beautiful—

Whose very faulterings groundward come of flight

Urged by a pinion all too passionate

For heaven and what it holds of gloom and glow :

Bravest of thinkers, bravest of the bràve

Doers, exalt in Science, rapturous

In Art, the—more than all—magnetic race

To fascinate their fellows, mould mankind

Hohenstiel-Schwangau-fashion,—these, what?—these

Will have to abdicate their primacy

Should such a nation sell them steel untaxed,

And such another take itself, on hire

For the natural sen'night, somebody for lord

Unpatronized by me whose back was turned ?

Or such another yet would fain build bridge,

Lay rail, drive tunnel, busy its poor self

With its appropriate fancy : so there 's—flash—

Hohenstiel-Schwangau up in arms at once !

Genius has somewhat of the infantine :

But of the childish, not a touch nor taint

Except through self-will, which, being foolishness,

Is certain, soon or late, of punishment.

Which Providence avert !—and that it may

Avert what both of us would so deserve,

No foolish dread o' the neighbour, I enjoin !

By consequence, no wicked war with him,

While I rule !

Does that mean—no war at all

When just the wickedness I here proscribe

Comes, haply, from the neighbour?   Does my speech

Precede the praying that you beat the sword

To plough-share, and the spear to pruning-hook,

And sit down henceforth under your own vine

And fig-tree through the sleepy summer month,

Letting what hurly-burly please explode

On the other side the mountain-frontier?   No,

Beloved! I foresee and I announce

Necessity of warfare in one case,

For one cause: one way, I bid broach the blood

O' the world.   For truth and right, and only right

And truth,—right, truth, on the absolute scale of God,

No pettiness of man's admeasurement,—

In such case only, and for such one cause,

Fight your hearts out, whatever fate betide

Hands energetic to the uttermost!

Lie not! Endure no lie which needs your heart

And hand to push it out of mankind's path—

No lie that lets the natural forces work

Too long ere lay it plain and pulverized—

Seeing man's life lasts only twenty years !

And such a lie, before both man and God,

Being, at this time present, Austria's rule

O'er Italy,—for Austria's sake the first,

Italy's next, and our sake last of all,

Come with me and deliver Italy !

Smite hip and thigh until the oppressor leave

Free from the Adriatic to the Alps

The oppressed one ! We were they who laid her low

In the old bad day when Villany braved Truth

And Right, and laughed 'Henceforward, God deposed,

The Devil is to rule for evermore

I' the world !'—whereof to stop the consequence,

17

And for atonement of false glory there

Gaped at and gabbled over by the world,

We purpose to get God enthroned again

For what the world will gird at as sheer shame

I' the cost of blood and treasure. 'All for nought—

Not even, say, some patch of province, splice

O' the frontier ?—some snug honorarium-fee

Shut into glove and pocketed apace ?'

(Questions Sagacity) 'in deference

To the natural susceptibility

Of folks at home, unwitting of that pitch

You soar to, and misdoubting if Truth, Right

And the other such augustnesses repay

Expenditure in coin o' the realm,—but prompt

To recognize the cession of Savoy

And Nice as marketable value !'   No,

Sagacity, go preach to Metternich,

And, sermon ended, stay where he resides !

Hohenstiel-Schwangau, you and I must march

The other road ! war for the hate of war,

Not love, this once !"   So Italy was free.

What else noteworthy and commendable

I' the man's career ?—that he was resolute

No trepidation, much less treachery

On his part, should imperil from its poise

The ball o' the world, heaved up at such expense

Of pains so far, and ready to rebound,

Let but a finger maladroitly fall,

Under pretence of making fast and sure

The inch gained by late volubility,

And run itself back to the ancient rest

At foot o' the mountain.   Thus he ruled, gave proof

The world had gained a point, progressive so,

By choice, this time, as will and power concurred,

O' the fittest man to rule ; not chance of birth,

Or such-like dice-throw.   Oft Sagacity

Was at his ear : " Confirm this clear advance,

Support this wise procedure !   You, elect

O' the people, mean to justify their choice

And out-king all the kingly imbeciles ; .

But that 's just half the enterprise : remains

You find them a successor like yourself,

In head and heart and eye and hand and aim,

Or all done 's undone ; and whom hope to mould

So like you as the pupil Nature sends,

The son and heir's completeness which you lack?

Lack it no longer!   Wed the pick o' the world,

Where'er you think you find it.   Should she be

A queen,—tell Hohenstielers-Schwangauese

' So do the old enthroned decrepitudes

Acknowledge, in the rotten hearts of them,

Their knell is knolled, they hasten to make peace

With the new order, recognize in me

Your right to constitute what king you will,

Cringe therefore crown in hand and bride on arm,

To both of us: we triumph, I suppose!'

Is it the other sort of rank?—bright eye,

Soft smile, and so forth, all her queenly boast?

Undaunted the exordium—'I, the man

O' the people, with the people mate myself:

So stand, so fall.   Kings, keep your crowns and brides !

Our progeny (if Providence agree)

Shall live to tread the baubles underfoot

And bid the scarecrows consort with their kin.

For son, as for his sire, be the free wife

In the free state !'

That is, Sagacity

Would prop up one more lie, the most of all

Pernicious fancy that the son and heir

Receives the genius from the sire, himself

Transmits as surely,—ask experience else !

Which answers,—never was so plain a truth

As that God drops his seed of heavenly flame

Just where He wills on earth : sometimes where man

Seems to tempt—such the accumulated store

Of faculties—one spark to fire the heap;

Sometimes where, fire-ball-like, it falls upon

The naked unpreparedness of rock,

Burns, beaconing the nations through their night.

Faculties, fuel for the flame?   All helps

Come, ought to come, or come not, crossed by chance,

From culture and transmission.   What's your want

I' the son and heir?   Sympathy, aptitude,

Teachableness, the fuel for the flame?

You 'll have them for your pains: but the flame's self,

The novel thought of God shall light the world ?

No, poet, though your offspring rhyme and chime

I' the cradle,—painter, no, for all your pet

Draws his first eye, beats Salvatore's boy,—

And thrice no, statesman, should your progeny

Tie bib and tucker with no tape but red,

And make a foolscap-kite of protocols !

Critic and copyist and bureaucrat

To heart's content !   The seed o' the apple-tree

Brings forth another tree which bears a crab :

'T is the great gardener grafts the excellence

On wildings where he will.

                  " How plain I view,

Across those misty years 'twixt me and Rome "—

(Such the man's answer to Sagacity)

· "The little wayside temple, half way down

To a mild river that makes oxen white

Miraculously, un-mouse-colours hide,

Or so the Roman country people dream !

I view that sweet small shrub-embedded shrine

On the declivity, was sacred once

To a transmuting Genius of the land,

Could touch and turn its dunnest natures bright,

—Since Italy means the Land of the Ox, we know.

Well, how was it the due succession fell

From priest to priest who ministered i' the cool

Calm fane o' the Clitumnian god ?   The sire

Brought forth a son and sacerdotal sprout,

Endowed instinctively with good and grace

To suit the gliding gentleness below—

Did he ?   Tradition tells another tale.

Each priest obtained his predecessor's staff,

Robe, fillet and insignia, blamelessly,

By springing out of ambush, soon or late,

And slaying him : the initiative rite

Simply was murder, save that murder took,

I' the case, another and religious name.

So it was once, is now, shall ever be

With genius and its priesthood in this world :

The new power slays the old—but handsomely.

There he lies, not diminished by an inch

Of stature that he graced the altar with,

Though somebody of other bulk and build

Cries 'What a goodly personage lies here

Reddening the water where the bulrush roots !

May I conduct the service in his place,

Decently and in order, as did he,

And, as he did not, keep a wary watch

When meditating 'neath a willow shade ! '

Find out your best man, sure the son of him,

Will prove best man again, and, better still

Somehow than best, the grandson-prodigy !

You think the world would last another day

Did we so make us masters of the trick

Whereby the works go, we could pre-arrange

Their play and reach perfection when we please ?

Depend on it, the change and the surprise

Are part o' the plan : 't is we wish steadiness ;

Nature prefers a motion by unrest,

Advancement through this force that jostles that.

And so, since much remains i' the world to see,

Here is it still, affording God the sight."

Thus did the man refute Sagacity,

Ever at this one whisper in his ear :

" Here are you picked out, by a miracle,

And placed conspicuously enough, folks say

And you believe, by Providence outright

Taking a new way—nor without success—

To put the world upon its mettle : good !

But Fortune alternates with Providence ;

Resource is soon exhausted.   Never count

On such a happy hit occurring twice !

Try the old method next time !"

" Old enough,"

(To whisper in his ear, the laugh outbroke)

" And most discredited of all the modes

By just the men and women who make boast

They are kings and queens thereby! Mere self-defence

Should teach them, on one chapter of the law

Must be no sort of trifling—chastity :

They stand or fall, as their progenitors

Were chaste or unchaste. Now, run eye around

My crowned acquaintance, give each life its look

And no more,—why, you 'd think each life was led

Purposely for example of what pains

Who leads it took to cure the prejudice,

And prove there 's nothing so unproveable

As who is who, what son of what a sire,

And,—inferentially,—how faint the chance

That the next generation needs to fear

Another fool o' the selfsame type as he

Happily regnant now by right divine

And luck o' the pillow !   No : select your lord

By the direct employment of your brains

As best you may,—bad as the blunder prove,

A far worse evil stank beneath the sun

When some legitimate blockhead managed so

Matters that high time was to interfere,

Though interference came from hell itself

And not the blind mad miserable mob

Happily ruled so long by pillow-luck

And divine right,—by lies in short, not truth.

And meanwhile use the allotted minute . . .

———

One,—

Two, three, four, five—yes, five the pendule warns!

Eh? Why, this wild work wanders past all bound

And bearing! Exile, Leicester-square, the life

I' the old gay miserable time, rehearsed,

Tried on again like cast clothes, still to serve

At a pinch, perhaps? "Who's who?" was aptly asked,

Since certainly I am not I! since when?

Where is the bud-mouthed arbitress? A nod

Out-Homering Homer! Stay—there flits the clue

I fain would find the end of! Yes,—" Meanwhile,

Use the allotted minute!" Well, you see,

(Veracious and imaginary Thiers,

Who map out thus the life I might have led,

But did not,—all the worse for earth and me—

Doff spectacles, wipe pen, shut book, decamp !)

You see 't is easy in heroics !   Plain

Pedestrian speech shall help me perorate.

Ah, if one had no need to use the tongue !

How obvious and how easy 't is to talk

Inside the soul, a ghostly dialogue—

Instincts with guesses,—instinct, guess, again

With dubious knowledge, half-experience : each

And all the interlocutors alike

Subordinating,—as decorum bids,

Oh, never fear ! but still decisively,—

Claims from without that take too high a tone,

—(" God wills this, man wants that, the dignity

Prescribed a prince would wish the other thing ")—

Putting them back to insignificance

Beside one intimatest fact—myself

Am first to be considered, since I live

Twenty years longer and then end, perhaps !

But, where one ceases to soliloquize,

Somehow the motives, that did well enough

I' the darkness, when you bring them into light

Are found, like those famed cave-fish, to lack eye

And organ for the upper magnitudes.

The other common creatures, of less fine

Existence, that acknowledge earth and heaven,

Have it their own way in the argument.

Yes, forced to speak, one stoops to say—one's aim

Was—what it peradventure should have been ;—

To renovate a people, mend or end

That bane come of a blessing meant the world—

Inordinate culture of the sense made quick

By soul,—the lust o' the flesh, lust of the eye,

And pride of life,—and, consequent on these,

The worship of that prince o' the power o' the air

Who paints the cloud and fills the emptiness

And bids his votaries, famishing for truth,

Feed on a lie.

           Alack, one lies oneself

Even in the stating that one's end was truth,

Truth only, if one states as much in words !

Give me the inner chamber of the soul

For obvious easy argument ! 't is there

One pits the silent truth against a lie—

Truth which breaks shell a careless simple bird,

Nor wants a gorget nor a beak filed fine,

Steel spurs and the whole armoury o' the tongue,

To equalize the odds.   But, do your best,

Words have to come : and somehow words deflect

As the best cannon ever rifled will.

So, i' the Residenz yet, not Leicester-square,

Alone,—no such congenial intercourse !—

My reverie concludes, as dreaming should, ·

With daybreak : nothing done and over yet,

Except cigars !   The adventure thus may be,

Or never needs to be at all : who knows?

My Cousin-Duke, perhaps, at whose hard head

—Is it, now—is this letter to be launched,

The sight of whose grey oblong, whose grim seal,

Set all these fancies floating for an hour?

Twenty years are good gain, come what come will!

Double or quits! The letter goes! Or stays?

THE END.

London: Printed by SMITH, ELDER & Co., Old Bailey, E.C.